WILD THINGS!

Elephant
in the attic

Lisa Regan

ILLUSTRATED BY **Kelly Caswell**

BLOOMSBURY

LONDON NEW DELHI NEW YORK SYDNEY

KU-719-045

Published 2013 by
Bloomsbury Publishing Plc
50 Bedford Square, London, WC1B 3DP

www.bloomsbury.com

ISBN   HB 978-1-4081-7937-6
       PB 978-1-4081-7938-3

Text copyright © 2013 Lisa Regan

The right of Lisa Regan to be identified as the author of this work has been asserted by her in accordance
with the Copyrights, Designs and Patents Act 1988.

Manufactured and supplied under licence from the Zoological Society of London.
Copyright © 2013. All rights reserved.

A CIP catalogue for this book is available from the British Library.

All rights reserved. No part of this publication may be reproduced in any form or by any means – graphic,
electronic or mechanical, including photocopying, recording, taping or information storage and retrieval
systems – without the prior permission in writing of the publishers.

Every effort has been made to trace copyright holders and to obtain their permission for use of copyright
material. The author and publishers would be pleased to rectify any error or omission in future editions.

This book is produced using paper that is made from wood grown in managed, sustainable forests.
It is natural, renewable and recyclable. The logging and manufacturing processes conform to the
environmental regulations of the country of origin.

Produced for Bloomsbury Publishing by Calcium. www.calciumcreative.co.uk

Illustrated by Kelly Caswell

Picture acknowledgements: Shutterstock: Ian Cook 23tl, Naas Rautenbach 23tr.

Printed in China by Toppan Leefung

All the internet addresses given in this book were correct at the time of going to press. The author and
publishers regret any inconvenience caused if addresses have changed or sites have ceased to exist,
but can accept no responsibility for any such changes.

HB 10 9 8 7 6 5 4 3 2 1
PB 10 9 8 7 6 5 4 3 2 1

MIX
Paper from
responsible sources
FSC
www.fsc.org   FSC® C104723

WAKEFIELD LIBRARIES & INFO. SERVICES	
30000010247614	
Bertrams	08/01/2013
J599.67	£8.99

Wakefield Libraries
& Information Services

Pontefract Library
Shoemarket
Pontefract
WF8 1BD

01977 727692

This book should be returned by the last date stamped above. You may renew the loan personally, by post or telephone for a further period if the book is not required by another reader.

WAKEFIELD LIBRARIES

30000010247614

Contents

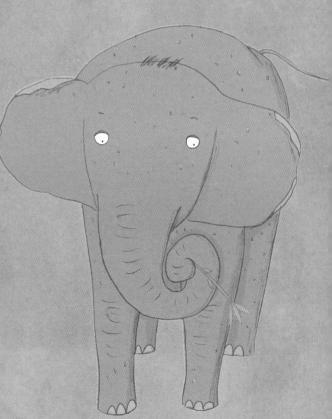

Ring, ring. Wild thing!

If you're WILD about animals, today's your lucky day.

There's an elephant at the door! You could invite it in...

Hello!

Male elephants live on their own.

6

A **herd** is made up of female **relatives** such as mums, aunts, and sisters.

Yikes!

Meet the family!

You will need

Lots of bedrooms

Plenty of food

7

Spray!

Elephants love to take a shower.

They use their trunks to suck up water. Then they spray it over their bodies.

You will need

A **hose** (if you want to join in)

8

Elephants then cover themselves in dust!

Cool!

Munch!

Elephants eat A LOT.

They are so big they need to eat all day long.

You will need

Grass, **roots**, **bark**, fruit – and lots of other stuff!

Err..?

There won't be much of your garden left.

11

Giant!

Elephants are the biggest animals on land.

They are taller than the first **storey** of a house.

Squeeze!

You will need

A lot of outside space!

Can't...quite...fit!

13

Trumpet!

An elephant's trumpeting noise is very LOUD.

It likes to be heard from a long way away.

Ouch!

Your pet's noise will really hurt your ears!

You will need

Earplugs for your family – and the whole of your street

Watch out!

A gentle elephant can become scary when it is cross.

Elephants stamp and **charge** to **protect** their babies.

Angry elephants can run really quickly.

Don't make, me mad!

You will need

To stay friends with your new guest

17

Time to go home

Your elephant seems happy, but your parents really aren't!

It's time to post your pet back to its real home...

A dog makes a great pet, but an elephant is a WILD THING!

19

Cool creatures

Elephants come from **Africa** and **Asia**. Asian elephants have smaller ears and bodies than African elephants.

Female elephants are called cows. Males are called bulls.

An adult Asian elephant can grow to more than 3 metres tall.

Male Asian elephants have tusks. These are long front teeth at the front of the elephant's mouth.

A herd of elephants is usually made up of between three and seven females from the same family.

To pick things up, an elephant can use its trunk like a hand. It can also use it like a hosepipe, to squirt water!

Glossary

Africa a large continent

Asia *the world's largest continent*

bark *the tough outside layer of a tree*

charge *to run quickly towards something*

earplugs *small, soft objects put in the ears
to keep out noise*

herd *a group of animals that live together*

hose *a long pipe used to spray water*

protect *to keep safe*

relatives *members of the same family*

roots *the parts of a plant or a tree that
grow into the ground and suck up water*

storey *one level of a building*

Thanks for having me!

The Zoological Society of
London (ZSL) is a charity
that provides help for animals
at home and worldwide. We also run
ZSL London Zoo and ZSL Whipsnade Zoo.

By buying this book, you have helped us raise money
to continue our work with animals around the world.

Find out more at zsl.org

ZSL
LIVING CONSERVATION

ZSL
LONDON
ZOO

ZSL
WHIPSNADE
ZOO

23

Take them all home!

ISBN HB 978-1-4081-7937-6
       PB 978-1-4081-7938-3

ISBN HB 978-1-4081-4247-9
       PB 978-1-4081-5678-0

ISBN HB 978-1-4081-4246-2
       PB 978-1-4081-5679-7

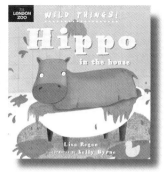

ISBN HB 978-1-4081-4245-5
       PB 978-1-4081-5680-3

ISBN HB 978-1-4081-4244-8
       PB 978-1-4081-5681-0

ISBN HB 978-1-4081-7939-0
       PB 978-1-4081-7940-6

ISBN HB 978-1-4081-7941-3
       PB 978-1-4081-7942-0

ISBN HB 978-1-4081-7935-2
       PB 978-1-4081-7936-9